CHURCH MEMBERSHIP
IN THE BIBLE

CHURCH MEMBERSHIP
in the Bible

PETER MASTERS

THE WAKEMAN TRUST, LONDON

CHURCH MEMBERSHIP IN THE BIBLE
This edition © Peter Masters 2008

THE WAKEMAN TRUST
(Wakeman Trust is a UK Registered Charity)

UK Registered Office
38 Walcot Square
London SE11 4TZ

USA Office
300 Artino Drive
Oberlin, OH 44074-1263
Website: www.wakemantrust.org

ISBN 978 1 870855 64 8

Cover design by Andrew Owen

Printed by Stephens & George, Merthyr Tydfil, UK

Contents

1
The Biblical Duty of Joining a Church

CHRIST HAS DESIGNED a 'home' or family for his people, described in these pages as an accomplishment of divine genius. This is a magnificent subject, vital to spiritual growth and blessing and also to our service for the Saviour. It is a subject enriched by remarkable 'church metaphors' or illustrations, so illuminating and so perfectly synchronising with each other. Next to having a real walk with Christ and knowing the doctrines of the faith, membership of a good church has a powerful formative influence on the believer's life.

So what should a biblical local church be like? And what are the duties of members? Some sincere Christians are not convinced of the need for church membership, while others simply let the years pass by without committing themselves to becoming part of a church. We begin, therefore, with the church organisation laid down by the apostles in obedience to the Lord – the pattern for us today.

Did believers of New Testament times actually join anything? Many passages in the New Testament use the unmistakable language of *belonging,* or membership. The local church is defined as a special unit or spiritual family designed and intended by God for joining, so that those who belong are pledged and committed to its purposes, life and discipline.

Insiders and outsiders

First, we learn from *1 Corinthians 5.4-5* that the local church of the first century was a properly constituted community with the power to exercise discipline. (The case in hand was the expulsion of a man for fornication.) In this passage Paul writes:

'In the name of our Lord Jesus Christ, when ye are gathered together, and my spirit, with the power of our Lord Jesus Christ, to deliver such an one unto Satan for the destruction of the flesh, that the spirit may be saved in the day of the Lord Jesus.'

This may, at first sight, seem a strange verse to prove the principle of church membership, but it is of great relevance for it describes how a special meeting of believers had the power to exclude from their company and privileges someone guilty of serious sin. This was obviously not merely a gathering, or an open public meeting, held at Corinth, including unbelievers and seekers. (*1 Corinthians 14.24-25* shows that unbelievers attended the ordinary public services of the church at Corinth.) It was very specifically a meeting of disciples or believers, concerned to guard the integrity of their association.

The Corinthian sinner was 'delivered unto Satan', which meant that he was deprived of the comforts and blessings of spiritual fellowship and made to live outside the community of believers, back in the world, in order to bring him to his senses, and to preserve the purity of the church. In *1 Corinthians 5.12-13* the apostle continues to use the powerful language of belonging, writing:–

'For what have I to do to judge them also that are without? do not ye judge them that are within? But them that are without God judgeth.'

Insiders? Outsiders? Insiders or outsiders of what? Of a gathering only, or of formal church membership? This kind of language can only refer to a definite church membership of professing Christians, for only such a company would have the authority of the Lord to judge the conduct of other Christians.

It is clear that a church in New Testament times was a defined circle of people that you could be received into, or put out of. The people in this company had voluntarily committed themselves to the mutual fellowship, service and discipline of their Christian community. They were no longer uncommitted individualists.

Christians who do not accept the biblical concept of church membership have to adopt a most improbable position in order to explain the passages just quoted. They have to interpret them as referring to attendance of the Lord's Supper, saying that the exclusion of the sinful man in Corinth was a ban on his attending the Lord's Table.

While Paul does mention the Lord's Supper, this is only part of his command. The instruction to 'purge out' *(1 Corinthians 5.7)* is not primarily a command to exclude someone from the Lord's Table, but to expel from the body. The same goes for Paul's phrase, 'put away' *(1 Corinthians 5.13)*[*] and it is obvious to us that when the apostle uses terms like 'without' and 'within' *(1 Corinthians 5.12)* he cannot mean the Lord's Table, but the *membership* of the church at Corinth.

Constituted for discipline

The necessity for a proper membership structure in local churches is seen also in *Matthew 18*, where the Lord Jesus Christ

---

[*] Paul actually quotes from *Deuteronomy 17.7*, which refers to evil being entirely put away from among God's people.

gives a general principle for dealing with offences among believers. This passage does not teach the detailed procedure for dealing with offences (for this is elaborated upon in the epistles), but it lays down the principle that when serious offences occur among the Lord's people which they cannot resolve, then the matter is to be dealt with *by the church*, and if the offender fails to heed the church, then he must suffer exclusion from its fellowship. The Lord says: 'And if he shall neglect to hear them, tell it unto the church: but if he neglect to hear the church, let him be unto thee as an heathen man and a publican.' The Saviour here puts into the hands of local churches a responsibility which proves beyond doubt that such churches should be stable, properly defined, constituted, orderly communities, not shapeless forms, with no specific membership.

Joining the church at Jerusalem

In the *Acts of the Apostles* we find several key references to joining a church, a significant example being *Acts 9.26-28*:

'And when Saul was come to Jerusalem, he assayed to join himself to the disciples: but they were all afraid of him, and believed not that he was a disciple. But Barnabas took him, and brought him to the apostles, and declared unto them how he had seen the Lord in the way, and that he had spoken to him, and how he had preached boldly at Damascus in the name of Jesus. And he was with them coming in and going out at Jerusalem.'

What exactly was Saul trying to join? Was he merely trying to attend the services of the congregation? This is surely wide of the mark, for he would not have been turned away from the preaching. The congregations of New Testament times showed outstanding courage in their public witness, and the sheer size of the Jerusalem gatherings would have made it very easy for anyone to be present at their public preaching services.

The fact that church members were afraid of Saul did not mean that they shut him out of their congregations. They were obviously doubtful of Saul in the context of close spiritual fellowship, and would not let him join them at that deeper level, although he tried to do so. Saul was attempting to join the membership of those who had professed Christ. The words of the record confirm this was the case by saying specifically that he attempted to join 'the disciples' – the term for the community of professing believers. It was only when Barnabas spoke for Saul before the leaders of the church that he was able to join them.

The joining verb – to glue

This brings us to a study of a vital term used in this and other passages of *Acts* – the word *join*. The Greek word literally means to *glue, stick* or *cement* two things together, and it always signifies a very close dependence or bond. The prodigal son, for example, is said to have *joined* himself, or glued himself, to a native of a far country for employment. Here the word describes a dependent, needy employee who pledges himself to obey his employer for money.

In *1 Corinthians 6.16* this same word (glued together) is used to describe sexual relationships, even sinful ones, and in *1 Corinthians 6.17* the word is used again to describe the deep bond of total commitment which marks a true Christian ('He that is joined unto the Lord is one spirit').

In *Acts 8.29*, Philip is told by the Holy Spirit to join himself (the same glue verb again) to the Ethiopian eunuch's chariot, which he did in a sense. He embarked on a determined witness and stuck tenaciously to that seeking nobleman until saving light dawned. The glue verb is only used in the New Testament to indicate a close, special obligation or commitment, and in every passage refers to a relationship which is mutual, both parties consenting.

Another example of the use of the glue verb is *Acts 5.12-14*. Following the judgement of Ananias and Sapphira, many people were put off joining the church. The passage reads:

'And by the hands of the apostles were many signs and wonders wrought among the people; (and they were all with one accord in Solomon's porch. And of the rest durst no man join himself to them: but the people magnified them. And believers were the more added to the Lord, multitudes both of men and women.)'

The crowds continued to turn out to the open air preaching places, such as Solomon's porch, but many were frightened of closer involvement after the incident with Ananias and Sapphira. There was a difference between being in the congregation and being glued or joined to the church. Such passages prove beyond doubt that the New Testament churches – our pattern for today – possessed a clear membership structure.

A definite organisation

We next look at a number of scriptures which only make sense if we accept that a church has a membership of truly and mutually committed members. *Ephesians 5.21* tells us we should always be – 'Submitting yourselves one to another in the fear of God'. This command implies that believers should see themselves as a community, and the community should come before individual whims and desires.

Galatians 2.4 uses the language of membership very clearly, Paul speaking – 'of false brethren unawares brought in, who came in privily *[ie: secretly, because they were not entitled to admission]* to spy out our liberty which we have in Christ Jesus, that they might bring us into bondage.' Here we discover that there was a meeting or gathering of Christians which not everyone in the public congregation was qualified to attend. Outsiders wishing to gain illicit entry would have to sneak in secretly. What could this be other than a gathering of the members? What other kind of meeting would some people not be entitled to attend?

There are many such texts which make no sense if the New Testament churches did not have a specific membership. Without church membership, for example, what would we make of

1 Timothy 3.1: 'This is a true saying, If a man desire the office of a bishop *[or overseer]*, he desireth a good work'? An overseer of what? Overseer means an inspector, or over-watcher, who has legitimate authority or care over others. The New Testament overseer is a church officer responsible for believers who have made themselves accountable to God and to the local church. The whole notion of oversight and government collapses without such a membership, and the Scripture cannot be obeyed.

Similarly, we see the necessity of church membership from the duties of the elder listed in *1 Timothy 3.5*. Consider Paul's statement: 'For if a man know not how to rule his own house, how shall he take care of the church of God?' The local church is like a family, and the responsibilities and duties of a father are very like those of the overseer to the church. A family is a cohesive unit with a unique bond between its members.

In *1 Timothy 5.17* we read, 'Let the elders that rule well...' Once again we must ask, how can there be 'rule' in a church which has no constituted membership? There could be no orderly oversight of a nation which had no proper citizens, an army without enlisted soldiers, an industry without employees, or a family without children. The will of God is clearly that there should be a spiritual family in which elders are responsible to nurture and help members, and members are responsible to pool their strengths and concern to the ministry of that family.

The great church metaphors

In addition to all these passages of Scripture, irrefutable arguments for the duty of church membership flow from the seven great church metaphors of the New Testament, illustrations used to describe churches. These are:

1. The Temple building
2. The body
3. The household or family

4. The vine

5. The flock

6. The bride

7. The priesthood

The first three church metaphors are used very specifically to describe an individual, local church, while the last four are more elastic, sometimes being used for the entire, universal church of Christ throughout time and eternity. The first three church metaphors demonstrate beyond all doubt that believers have an obligation to seek church membership, and that membership involves a real pledge and commitment to the church. It involves a humble acceptance and support of the doctrines, discipline and service of a particular congregation.

The building metaphor

The illustration of the building (usually the Temple) appears in several scriptures. *Ephesians 2.21-22* reads: 'In whom all the building fitly framed together groweth unto an holy temple in the Lord: in whom ye also are builded together for an habitation of God through the Spirit.' A building is, of course, a unity of parts, whether of stones or bricks or timbers.

If there was no membership, if every man did that which was right in his own eyes, if everyone decided to carry out whatever form of Christian testimony he wished to engage in, then the Temple picture would be irrelevant, for it cannot depict anarchy and individualism. But the Lord, who has fashioned and made every believer physically, mentally and spiritually, has also designed a place for each one. Just as stones, beams, columns, timbers, lintels and other parts are firmly placed in their correct, pre-planned positions in a fine building, the Lord calls his people into membership together, to be used by him, under the guidance of the Holy Spirit. There is a wonderful orderliness about the local church, as designed and intended by God.

1 Timothy 3.15 also describes membership in a very powerful way:

'That thou mayest know how thou oughtest to behave thyself in the house of God, which is the church of the living God, the pillar and ground of the truth.' Once again the local church is compared to a physical building which has a foundation together with columns to support it. Like the Temple building with all its teaching in symbols, the members support and represent the Truth itself. Their conduct should honour such an illustration, which means that each member is to be a significant, stable, loadbearing part of the building. No Christian should be a free agent, a non-member. Walls and window frames do not drift in and out of a building.

The body metaphor

The body illustration is also found in a number of passages such as *1 Corinthians 12.12*: 'For as the body is one, and hath many members, and all the members of that one body, being many, are one body: so also is Christ.' A local church is seen here as very similar to a human body, a unit, having parts which are organically attached to it. They cannot fly away, nor do they have an intermittent attachment, but are firmly connected, contributing to and depending upon the whole unit. There is co-ordination and agreement between all the parts. The illustration is profound and establishes the necessity of membership in a particular church, involving close care and co-operation between its members.

We are taught that a congregation is far more than a number of people listening to the same preacher. It is a company in which all members have significant roles, and all depend in some respect on fellow members. There is order and a common direction. The head of the body is Christ, and him alone. (There are no archbishops or popes in the Bible.)

Ephesians 4.15-16 extends this illustration. Paul prays that believers – 'speaking the truth in love, may grow up into him in all things, which is the head, even Christ: from whom the whole body fitly joined together and compacted by that which every joint supplieth, according to the effectual working in the measure of every part, maketh increase of the body unto the edifying of itself in love.' One reason why God joins his people together in any church is so that every one may be involved in the growth of the body, by the witness of life and lip.

Is it possible that a limb or any other part of a body could ever be disconnected and kept alive and functioning usefully apart from the body? We conclude that a Christian can no more opt out of being a church member. Is there any provision in the New Testament for someone who does not wish to be a church member? The answer is: only if that person has to be expelled from a church for serious sin, or unbelief of the doctrines cherished by that church. There is no other circumstance in the New Testament in which a believer should not be a church member.

The family metaphor

Supposing someone were to say, 'But I think I am too young in the faith to be a church member.' We would immediately look to the metaphor of the family *(1 Timothy 3.5)*, observing that no one is too young to be in a family. It would never be suggested that a tiny baby is too young to be a member of a family household, and should be left on the doorstep. Being weak and vulnerable qualifies the baby all the more for special family care. The family metaphor does not require church membership for literal babies, but it does for spiritual babes.

A household, of course, is based on love, co-operation, order, headship, and common purpose. Its members have a deep interest in each other's spiritual well-being because they share the same name and filial bond. We, as born-again believers, are commanded by our Saviour to join ourselves to his people in church membership. It is obvious that the church we join should be completely committed to the infallible, inspired Word of God, and striving to fulfil the biblical pattern for Christ's churches summarised in the following pages.

2
The Character of a Local Church

THE NEW TESTAMENT teaches four basic principles which define and determine the character of individual churches of Christ, and which make them fully effective and well pleasing to him.

1. Christ is the Lord and Head of every individual local church, each one being entirely independent and autonomous, and not subject to any other church body, or 'hierarchy' of denominational authority.

2. Only born-again believers should be admitted into the membership of such a church; the principle of a regenerate church membership.

3. Every church member is to be sincerely and wholly committed in fellowship and service to the local church.

4. Every individual church living in obedience to the Lord should experience growth as a sign of spiritual life, subject to his will and timescale.

(1) The Independence of Each Congregation

We have stated that each church must be independent or autonomous, having no rule from any other church or inter-church hierarchy. (A proper temporary exception may come in the case of a 'daughter' church or mission, being founded by another.) Each local church should be under the direct government, guidance and blessing of Christ. Sadly, human schemes of church government have frequently neglected the biblical pattern, and devised centralised control over groups of churches, making it easy for Satan to corrupt the entire group, this being the story of historic denominations.

Here is the biblical evidence for the autonomy of a local church.* The New Testament epistles are addressed to local churches, or local pastors and office bearers, and worded in such a manner as to leave us in no doubt that those churches were independent of any central organisation. Each was individually answerable to God. Each owed allegiance and obedience directly to Christ. It has often been observed that Christ never founded a unifying organisation of churches, and when he speaks to churches he directly addresses each one, saying for example (in *Revelation 2.1*) − 'Unto the angel *[probably the minister]* of the church of Ephesus write; These things saith he that holdeth the seven stars in his right hand, who walketh in the midst of the seven golden candlesticks.'

---

* The term 'local church' has sometimes been misunderstood, and people have gained the impression that they should always seek membership at the very nearest evangelical church to their home. However, the term is not intended to refer to the nearness of the building to a believer's home. It simply describes an individual congregation, as distinct from the Church universal, or any group of churches. It describes a congregation worshipping and working under the direct rule of the Lord. In today's urbanised world believers cannot always live in the immediate vicinity of their church for a variety of reasons.

The candlesticks (or better – the lampstands) represent the churches *(Revelation 1.20)*, and the Lord is shown dealing directly with each one to challenge, encourage, or chastise. No bishop, archbishop, area superintendent, synod or such-like intervene, but Christ is the Lord of each individual fellowship to govern, empower and control, by his Word.

For practical confirmation of this principle we refer to *Acts 13.1-2*: 'Now there were in the church that was at Antioch certain prophets and teachers…As they ministered to the Lord, and fasted, the Holy Ghost said, Separate me Barnabas and Saul for the work whereunto I have called them.' Most of the apostles were at that time resident with the church at Jerusalem, but here is an example of how the Holy Spirit went directly to the church at Antioch, not via the church at Jerusalem. Antioch is seen as an independent church being separately governed and guided by the Lord, without human inter-church hierarchy of any kind.

The importance of the individual church being directly accountable to Christ is confirmed from the way the word for church is used in the New Testament. The Greek word is *ekklesia* meaning *called out, summoned out* or *gathered*, to form an assembly. It occurs in the New Testament 114 times, and is not once used to describe a national church, or any other group of churches. We emphasise, the Scripture never graces a group of churches with this key word – 'church'.

The *ekklesia* word is used in four out of every five references to describe an individual local community of Christian people meeting in a certain town or place. In one out of every five references the word is used to describe the entire elect of God, the invisible church made up of believers from every age and every nation. Mostly, therefore, it is applied to single congregations (eg: 'Greet the *church* that is in their house'), and sometimes to the church universal, but never to anything in between. Knowledge of these things helps us to see the very great significance of each individual, local church in the New Testament.

Today the word *church* is used very clumsily, and people speak of all Christians in a particular country as 'the church' there. The Bible never does this. If Christians spread over a region are referred to, it speaks of 'the churches' in the plural. There are 35 such references, an example being *1 Corinthians 14.34,* 'Let your women keep silence in the churches.'

The church metaphors referred to earlier also demonstrate that each individual church is supposed to be directly answerable to God, especially the metaphors of the body, the Temple and the family. Each human body is quite separate from any other body and is directed from its own head. The head of the body (see *Ephesians 4.15*) is Christ, while the body stands for the local church. Therefore each local church is directly under Christ. This church illustration has no room for a man-made hierarchy or national church.

The Temple building is another illustration of the local church *(1 Corinthians 3.9-17).* The foundation of this local church is Christ (verse 11), who is also the chief cornerstone *(Ephesians 2.20-22).* In other words, every local church rests directly upon Christ.

The family is also a picture of the local church, and we are sons and daughters of the living God. Each family is a self-contained unit living in intimate, close, affectionate relationship with its father. In exactly this sense every individual church enjoys the direct fatherly care of the Lord. If we cannot remember the Bible verses, we may remember the pictures which God has given us in his Word.

(2) Only Converted Members

The second principle which determines the character of Bible churches is that membership must be restricted to people who have a credible profession of faith. The rule that each church should have a regenerate membership was taken for granted in the epistles of the New Testament. This is demonstrated by the way Paul addresses churches in his epistles, writing to the Romans: 'To all that be in Rome, beloved of God, called to be saints: Grace to you and peace...'

(Romans 1.7). The apostle says the same to the church at Corinth, assuming that their membership was made up entirely of those who had found the Lord by a true spiritual experience: 'Unto the church of God which is at Corinth, to them that are sanctified in Christ Jesus, called to be saints...' *(1 Corinthians 1.2)*.

The opening greeting of *Colossians* also leaves us in no doubt that this church had a converted church membership: 'To the saints and faithful brethren in Christ which are at Colosse...' *(Colossians 1.2)*. Final confirmation of the aim to have as members only saved people is seen in *Acts 2.47* where it is recorded that 'the Lord added to the church *[at Jerusalem]* daily such as should be saved.'

The main objection to this teaching made by those who wish to justify a mixed church membership, including members who lack any evangelical profession of faith or clear conversion experience, is to say that it is impossible to achieve purity in a church, and it is therefore foolish to attempt it. Many people have pointed out that this argument could equally be applied to the duty of holiness, with disastrous results. Our assignment is to obey the pattern of the New Testament, not to succumb to weak human reasoning.

There is, however, a Scripture passage cited in support of a mixed church membership, this being the parable of the wheat and tares, beginning in *Matthew 13.24*. Great stress is laid on the fact that in the parable the servants are prevented from rooting up the tares from the field lest the wheat be rooted up also, and the conclusion is made – don't aim at a wholly converted membership. The householder of the parable says, 'Let both grow together until the harvest: and in the time of harvest I will say to the reapers, Gather ye together first the tares, and bind them in bundles to burn them: but gather the wheat into my barn.'

The question is – what does the field represent in this parable? Those who seek to justify a mixed membership in a church say that it represents the church. But Christ told the disciples – 'The field is the world.' This parable, therefore, does not teach that wheat and tares (saved and unsaved) must grow together in the *churches*, but that both will survive in the *world* until the time of judgement. It does not contradict the clear teaching of the texts we have reviewed, which insist upon a regenerate church membership.

To dispel any final doubts on this principle we only have to think of the great church metaphors and once again we are confronted by illustrations which perfectly fit the case. Think, first, of the illustration of the body. Every part of a body is alive; the body cannot accept dead limbs or parts. The idea that a church can consist of those who are born again and those who are not just does not fit the body metaphor.

The only New Testament church illustration which could appear to allow spiritually dead members is that of the building, being composed of inert materials. But in this case the Bible is careful to qualify the picture, stressing that church members are living stones *(1 Peter 2.5)*. There are no spiritually lifeless stones in this temple.

The metaphor of the family quite obviously does not countenance 'dead' members, but only living members, related to the Head of the family – the Lord Jesus. All the other church metaphors also cry out for a regenerate church membership, such as the illustration of the vine and its branches, where all the branches must have the same living character as the vine, those that fail to bear fruit being taken away *(John 15.2)*.

Our conclusion is: what kind of church should a born-again believer join? Spiritually, one which consists of saved people. The Lord has decreed that only truly converted believers should make up the membership of a local church.

(3) Wholly Committed Members

The third essential principle which should determine the character of a true church of Christ is that the members are to be of one mind, united in doctrine, learning the Word, zealously working together for the Lord, and seeking to increase in love for each other. In other words this is the principle of total commitment in fellowship and service.

Some Christians may question the need for a member to be so deeply attached to their church, feeling that to attend, worship, give to the work, and relate cordially should be enough. However, churches were never designed to be just a pulpit and an audience, but active, living bodies with each member sincerely involved in their ministry, as we see in the words of *Romans 12.1* – 'I beseech you therefore, brethren, by the mercies of God, that ye present your bodies a living sacrifice, holy, acceptable unto God, which is your reasonable service.' *Romans 12* is about the conduct of members in the church,[*] and sets out the minimum standards of church membership. It makes vital reading for church members.

Paul makes a powerful observation on the life of the church in Colosse when he writes – 'For though I be absent in the flesh, yet am I with you in the spirit, joying and beholding your order, and the stedfastness of your faith in Christ' *(Colossians 2.5)*. The word translated *order* means their *arrangement*, or (as in an army) their orderly ranks as they march, and their officer structure. The word shows that the Colossian church was ordered in the beautiful sense that everyone had a definite place or position in its ministry. The church resembled a battalion of the Lord's army with everyone ready and occupying some vital position in the battle plan. Paul drew attention to the total engagement of the Colossian membership in the work of the Lord, whereby every man, woman and young person was striving in the work of the fellowship, all their gifts being exercised under mutual concern for effectiveness.

This principle of total, wholehearted commitment to a church is not an isolated teaching in the New Testament, because the church

---

[*] 'For as we have many members in one body, and all members have not the same office: so we, being many, are one body in Christ, and every one members one of another' *(Romans 12.4-5)*.

metaphors all stress this also. What kind of unity and integration exists in the body? It is a highly co-ordinated structure, in which eye and hand work together. It is a picture of great unity and inter-dependence of the parts. (See *1 Corinthians 12.13-27*.)

The building illustration repeats the lesson, for the stones of the Temple must be 'fitly framed together', interlocking closely so that the arches and vaults successfully support the building. Again, it is a picture of totally pooled effort and resources on the part of church members.

The vine picture also shows the intended character of a New Testament church, for in *John 15* we are taught that the very notion of dead, inactive branches is offensive to the Lord.

The family illustration gives a picture of the local church as a community of thriving members exercising real mutual care and sharing the breadwinning chores and other aims of the household.

Together the church metaphors lay upon us an obligation to relate closely to each other in the total worship and work effort of our fellowship. To be withdrawn, aloof, reserved, lazy, complacent or indifferent is a rejection of all the Lord's teaching on this subject.

(4) The Glory of Living Growth

The fourth essential which determines the character of Christ's churches is the principle of growth, experienced by all that live in obedience to his commands, and in accordance with the great commission of *Matthew 28.19-20*:

'Go ye therefore, and teach all nations, baptizing them in the name of the Father, and of the Son, and of the Holy Ghost: teaching them to observe all things whatsoever I have commanded you: and, lo, I am with you alway, even unto the end of the world. Amen.'

The extent to which we are able to make disciples may vary from generation to generation according to the sovereign will of God. Some believers will live in times of great reformation and revival, while others will live in days marked by militant resistance to the

Truth. We bear fruit 'some an hundredfold, some sixty, some thirty' *(Matthew 13.23)*; the quantity is with the Lord. But whether we are harvesting bountifully or struggling for small fruit, there will always be a harvest of souls to the Lord's churches. While we are endeavouring to make disciples, Christ is with us.

In taking encouragement from this teaching, we naturally allow for periods of sowing, for the Lord taught that making disciples is to be compared with sowing seed *(Matthew 13.3)*. The illustration of seedtime and harvest warns us that there will often be seasons of sowing and waiting, but harvest will follow, 'for in due season we shall reap, if we faint not' *(Galatians 6.9)*. The apostle Paul said to the Corinthians about his own preaching at Corinth, and the work of his successor, 'I have planted, Apollos watered; but God gave the increase' *(1 Corinthians 3.6)*.

Whether great or small, growth is an essential manifestation of life in a local Gospel church fulfilling the great commission, and the church metaphors again confirm the principle. In the illustration of the body, for example, *Ephesians 4.16* makes it very clear that a growing body is in mind. In the illustration of the building, we find that this also is a growing building; one in the course of construction and rising all the time *(Ephesians 2.21)*. And nothing speaks of growth like the family. Similarly, the flock is constantly being gathered, and the vine, like all plants, is never stationary, but growth and fruitbearing are fundamental to its life. In practically every church metaphor there is a very obvious reference to growth, development and extension, confirming to us that God's will is that his local churches should always be in a state of sowing and reaping the great harvest of souls.

The church a Christian must join should know these four great fundamental characteristics of a true Gospel church.

3
Purposes of the Local Church

THE FOUR PRINCIPLES just reviewed shape the character of an individual, local church. Next we consider the precise *purposes* of such a church. *Acts 2.41-47* is a passage that includes all the purposes of a local church, and these, for ease of reference, have been grouped under the four headings which follow.

The purposes of the local church are:

1. To engage in corporate worship.
2. To be a colony of Heaven on earth in fellowship and care.
3. To make known the glory of God through evangelism and the teaching of the Word.
4. To be the means by which believers pool their gifts and resources in God's service.

(1) Corporate Worship

The first purpose of a local church is to facilitate corporate worship, a duty and delight emphasised from *Genesis* to *Revelation*. The glory of corporate worship is that it will be continued as the greatest theme of eternity, when the redeemed will join with the angelic host in ascribing blessing, and honour, and glory, and power to the triune Godhead for ever and ever.

The glory of praise is to be found in its depth and sincerity, but also in the people of God joining together with heart and voice. Reverent praise, reading of Scripture, prayer and proclamation of the Word are the special work of a true church, which must provide an orderly, harmonious, congregational means of worship.

Corporate worship is also a very powerful witness. Worship that will impress the unconverted cannot normally spring from the devotions of an individual believer, because such worship is a private, intimate activity. Indeed, praying and almsgiving in public by individuals was not favoured by the Lord because of the problem of human pride. But the worship of a company of believers is (or should be) a public and a supremely humble activity. The fact that a company of people are seen heart and soul committed to the Lord, adoring and revering him as though they felt and sensed his presence and benefited from his power and glory – all this is a powerful witness.

We can see that certain practical duties as church members are involved in this. To worship God worthily we should be early settled and spiritually prepared for the worship services. We should have resolved our problems, confessed our sin before the Lord, and prepared our hearts for praise.

(2) A Colony of Heaven Uniquely Governed

The second purpose of a local church is to be as far as possible a colony of Heaven on earth, a faithful family of people who love Christ, reflect his character and ways, and prove his power and grace. It is the will of God that his people should be formed into families which exhibit all the beauty of unity, love and affection. A local church is intended to be something wonderful, exhibiting life and energy, and with its members supporting one another and caring for each other.

In this respect a local church is intended to be a powerful testimony, as the Saviour prayed in *John 17*, asking that we all may be one that the world may know the Truth. This oneness is not about uniting denominations, but about true Christians having common Christlike characteristics and biblical beliefs. Alongside evangelism, the outstanding character of the local church is intended to make a deep impression upon all who have opportunity to see its life and deportment. In *1 Peter 2.9* we are taught that we are – 'A chosen generation, a royal priesthood, an holy nation, a peculiar people; that ye should shew forth the praises *[or virtues]* of him who hath called you out of darkness into his marvellous light.'

Church members of New Testament times certainly saw themselves as a colony of Heaven. *Ephesians 2.19-22* expresses this: 'Ye are ... fellowcitizens with the saints, and of the household of God ... in whom ye also are builded together for an habitation of God through the Spirit.'

In order to accomplish and maintain such a beautiful and happy communion, the Lord has given congregations a pattern of order and government, particularly revealed in the pastoral epistles,[*] where many verses speak about rule, oversight and office bearers.

In the world we see a variety of systems of government, but the form given by the Lord for his churches is leadership by consent, in which the officers are elected by the members, and commanded to 'rule' by the Scripture and by their godly example.

There is a wonderful balance in scriptural church government, which is best appreciated by first drawing attention to its apparent contradiction. On the one hand the New Testament contains a group of Scripture passages which we may call the church meeting texts. These make the whole membership of a church responsible

---

[*] *1* and *2 Timothy* and *Titus*.

for deciding certain matters in its church meeting. These matters include, for example, the expenditure of large sums of money, the approval of stewardship accounts, the appointing of church officers and missionaries, and the receiving in and expelling of members.

However, there is another group of Scripture passages which at first sight seems to be in conflict with the first group. In these, church members are urged to subordinate themselves to and follow leaders who rule and who watch for souls. These are appointed by the members to lead and guide the affairs of the church, and are also given special responsibilities for discipline.

These two groups of texts are not actually in conflict. Taken together they show that all the members of a church are involved together in certain great decisions, while churches should cleave to the principle of being led by God's appointed office bearers for most other matters. One of the ways in which a local church succeeds in being a colony of Heaven is that there is this careful balance of leadership and total responsibility.

The local church does not have an autocratic leadership of office bearers who behave as 'lords over God's heritage', but a leadership within the family, which must commend itself to the family and prove itself. The officers of the church lead and guide in such a way as to carry the whole family of God in one grand spiritual objective and interest. It is a system of sympathetic leadership, a leadership from within rather than from above, and therefore a leadership in example and identification with the body.

We see the balance of this leadership in the church meeting, when rightly conducted. The business which is brought to a church meeting is not the petty, small, day-to-day affairs which should be entirely dealt with by officers. The members meet to receive new members, appoint office bearers, and to consider major projects, endeavours and expenses. The whole fellowship needs to share, endorse and be committed to these in prayer, stewardship and labour. In all such matters proposals should be brought to the church members' meeting by the leadership, for to have any other procedure would be to set aside all the leadership scriptures.

To be a colony of Heaven also means fulfilling all the duties of fellowship, love, friendship, mutual admonition, and the bearing of one another's burdens according to the law of Christ *(Galatians 6.2)*. These are set out later in this book (pages 37-45). Our calling as church members is to sow friendships, maintaining sensitivity to one another's needs, to be concerned and prayerful for each other, and to be as outgoing and unselfish as possible.

We have to avoid the temptation of using the Lord's church for our own pleasure and comfort, especially when young. Sometimes churches succumb to excessive fellowship and recreational activities, so that these become more significant than worship and spiritual advance. The church thus becomes a most congenial environment for Christianised pleasure, whereas we are all supposed to be sowing to the Spirit and asking ourselves, 'What do I contribute?'

(3) Proclamation of the Word

The third purpose of a local church (these purposes are not listed in order of priority) is to evangelise and teach the Word, and so to represent God in the world, and be 'the pillar and ground of the truth' *(1 Timothy 3.15)*. We see the church at Jerusalem engaging in vigorous personal witness and preaching, and in the study of the Word. The Pentecost sermon of Peter was a call to repentance and salvation *(Acts 2.38, 40)*, leading to fervent soul-winning activity by preachers and witnessing believers, so that 'daily in the temple, and in every house, they ceased not to teach and preach Jesus Christ' *(Acts 5.42)*. From the beginning the commission of the Lord began to be obeyed: 'Go ye into all the world, and preach the gospel to every creature' *(Mark 16.15)*.

To evangelise and teach the Word requires the organisation of churches, both for supporting preachers, using all capabilities, and caring for converts. These goals cannot be accomplished without local churches – Christ's appointed units for the work of the kingdom.

Each purpose of the local church so far considered represents activities which cannot be efficiently carried out without the church. It is very obvious that corporate worship cannot be offered without a gathering of people. Similarly there could be no colony of Heaven on earth, with its manifestation of spiritual *family* character, without such communities. And we could never effectively evangelise and care for converts without churches.

(4) Pooling of Resources

The fourth purpose of a local church is to pool the resources of Christian people for Christ's service, potentiating the abilities of church members and co-ordinating their efforts. This includes the training up of a succeeding generation of the Lord's people *(2 Timothy 2.2)*. These things cannot be done effectively without the local church. Christian people cannot pool their resources unless there is some blending unit. Nor can they have their abilities recognised, trained, refined and applied without mutual help. We return to the key text of *Ephesians 4.15-16*, complex and yet so perfect in speaking of the united labours of a company of God's people in his service. Paul prays that as church members we, 'speaking the truth in love, may grow up into him in all things, which is the head, even Christ: from whom the whole body fitly joined together and compacted by that which every joint supplieth, according to the effectual working in the measure of every part, maketh increase of the body unto the edifying of itself in love.'

Let us suppose that we all behaved as individualists and ignored church membership. Someone is extremely good at visitation, but much less effective at explaining the Gospel or counselling those with difficulties. It is clear that such a person, working by himself, will soon be in great difficulty. But his particular gift will be potentiated and greatly used in harmony with those of others if he is working in a fellowship of God's people, for others will do the preaching and counselling.

Our individual capacities, natural and spiritual, can only be brought to maximum usefulness if we are working together. The task of the local church, therefore, is to pool all our resources and our different gifts to make one, cohesive, complete, combined effort for the Lord – a working church. It is an inescapable fact that most of us, if we were not in a live fellowship of fellow workers, would soon become discouraged and despondent, and the forces against us would overpower us.

The stewardship of our means is also included in this function of the local church, for here we pool our financial resources to support the full-time ministry and many other needs. The main passage of

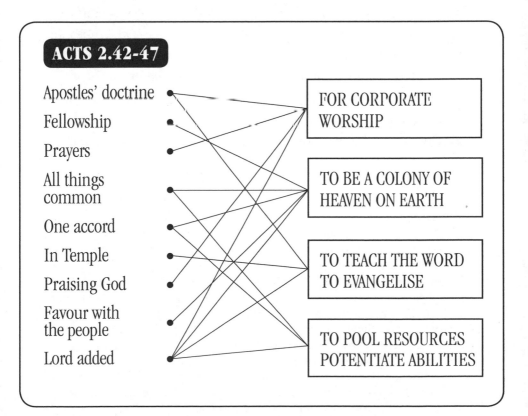

Scripture commanding this is *1 Corinthians 9.6-14.*[*]

It is clear that there is a great deal of organisation to be done in a local church to do justice to the abilities of all the members, although we always keep in mind that our human organisation amounts to nothing without the work of the Holy Spirit. As Charles Wesley wrote –

> *Except thou, Lord, shalt bless the plan,*
> *Our best conducted schemes are vain,*
>   *And never can succeed;*
> *We'll spend our utmost strength for nought,*
> *But if in thee our works are wrought,*
>   *They shall be blessed indeed.*

Satan will see to it that preachers and church leaders are tempted to retreat from these complex duties, and lapse into a simple preacher-congregation format, where no organisation or co-ordination of the service of all believers is necessary. As long as a few people can be found to run the Sunday School and other basic church departments there will be a minimum of 'fuss'. Satan will ensure that we view with dismay the struggle to make the largest possible outreach to the community, and to stir up the whole fellowship to constant activity, and find it too daunting to contemplate. However, we must

---

[*] 'Or I only and Barnabas, have not we power to forbear working? Who goeth a warfare any time at his own charges? who planteth a vineyard, and eateth not of the fruit thereof? or who feedeth a flock, and eateth not of the milk of the flock? Say I these things as a man? or saith not the law the same also? For it is written in the law of Moses, Thou shalt not muzzle the mouth of the ox that treadeth out the corn. Doth God take care for oxen? Or saith he it altogether for our sakes? For our sakes, no doubt, this is written: that he that ploweth should plow in hope; and that he that thresheth in hope should be partaker of his hope. If we have sown unto you spiritual things, is it a great thing if we shall reap your carnal things? If others be partakers of this power over you, are not we rather? Nevertheless we have not used this power; but suffer all things, lest we should hinder the gospel of Christ. Do ye not know that they which minister about holy things live of the things of the temple? and they which wait at the altar are partakers with the altar? Even so hath the Lord ordained that they which preach the gospel should live of the gospel.'

strive to honour this fourth purpose of a local church: the pooling of resources, the potentiating of abilities, and the formation of a real local unit of the Lord's army.

One of the great benefits of the local church, as opposed to some centralised national organisation, is that it minimises pride and the disease of 'establishmentitis'. The human mind is so weak (even among saved people) that it is very vulnerable at this point. Certain people love to have a large constituency or following, and then they lord it over their organisation. They develop a fear of being displaced, and resist others whose abilities may seem to threaten their own. They become intensely protective of their denomination or organisation, and when wrongs enter, there is no self-examination or challenge. Therefore these groupings become prime targets for contamination by Satan with false teachings and unbiblical methods. Consequently, denominations and centralised groupings have one after another fallen from their original soundness. This is an unassailable fact of history.

The local church, by contrast, is a creation of divine genius. The Lord Jesus Christ has swept complex human organisations of churches aside, and ordained only individual local churches. There should never be anything more complicated than a local church, for the Lord has decreed that his office bearers will be chosen by and function among people who know them intimately, and will not let them get 'too big for their boots', thus preserving them from establishment mentality.

This is just one reason why we admire the wonder of the New Testament pattern, and stay within the limits of the local church, not building great denominations and worldly-wise organisations which bring the very worst out of people, and always lead to disaster. The local church is a family of people saved and drawn together by the Lord for the pooling of their gifts and resources for his glorious service.

4
Loyalty to the Local Church

This chapter is taken from the author's volume *Steps for Guidance.* It is included here because it presents the very heart of belonging to a church, while also dealing with difficulties that may be found in a church.

ONE OF THE GREATEST problems reported in the life of local churches today is the lack of a deep sense of loyalty on the part of many members. Sometimes when believers decide where they would like to live, or where they will apply for new jobs, almost the last matter put into the reckoning is their commitment to their church. Pastors everywhere affirm that Christians are too often guided by material and personal considerations, and not by any sense of duty and loyalty to their fellowship.

Is it possible that our criteria for such decisions are out of line with the Lord's? What if he wants our present church commitment to be a dominating priority, and we relegate it to a matter of small importance? Will this not make all ideas of guidance an empty delusion? Clearly, it is vital for us to know the 'rating' our existing church commitment should be given on our scale of priorities. This chapter will show that some of the other guidance factors are subservient to this.

The writer knows of a 'pioneer' church where some years ago nine or ten couples committed themselves together to establish a witness in a new town destitute of evangelical light. Within three years, all but two of the couples had moved off elsewhere. The reason? Most had moved to get higher status and more lucrative jobs within their professions. Apparently these moves were not all absolutely essential, but the free choice of people who felt no deep bond of loyalty to the local 'body of Christ' in which God had placed them. Even though it seemed inevitable that their leaving would press their fledgling church to the brink of disaster, these couples considered their careers and incomes their chief priority.

A 'low' or 'high' view of the church?

How have such believers come to regard their ties with their local church so lightly? Obviously they have not really understood the Bible's teaching about the local church. Perhaps they have not realised what is meant by 'the body of Christ'. They think that the church is like a supermarket chain, or a network of banks. No one would decide against moving from one town to another because they were rather attached to their supermarket or bank branch. Suitable facilities exist almost wherever they may go.

What is the local church in our estimation? Is it merely a company of Christians conveniently gathered together for worship and instruction, or is it something special in God's sight? Has God chosen its members, organised the distribution of gifts and abilities, and called those individuals to be committed to each other to serve him and to live as a unique family? Does God require a special loyalty within the local church?

Liberty is the 'in' word today. For some believers, loyalty to any particular congregation smacks of restriction, legalism, and a mechanical interpretation of Christian duty. Loyalty is regarded as quenching the spirit of liberty. Yet the New Testament is clear in its portrayal of the local church as a company of believers very strongly related together in bonds of love *and loyalty* and service. The local church is much greater than a haphazard collection of believers. It is a spiritually integrated family vested with unique privileges and authority to carry out the commands of its Head, the Lord Jesus Christ. A local church is the object of his delight, and he is especially protective towards it.

The local church is – as Paul says repeatedly in *1 Corinthians 12 – one body*. In the eighteenth verse he says, 'Now hath God set the members every one of them in the body, as it hath pleased him.' In other words, God has designed each congregation. Paul goes on to say – 'There should be no schism in the body.' He then says that God has organised the distribution of capacities so that every member is of importance to the body. We therefore conclude that if any are removed, other than by the design and overruling of the Lord, some vital quality will be missing. The members care and feel for one another to the extent that when one suffers, all the others suffer also (verses 25-26). The *congregation* has a special place in the purposes of God.

We have seen already how *Ephesians 4.16* describes the organic unity of the congregation using the most close-knit illustration available – that of the physical body. Under the direction of the Head – 'the whole body fitly joined together and compacted by that which every joint supplieth, according to the effectual working in the measure of every part, maketh increase of the body unto the edifying of itself in love.'

The idea of joints and limbs being freely interchangeable between different bodies is unthinkable. The notion that a knuckle or elbow could unilaterally migrate to another body is ludicrous. The illustration of the body shows how seriously God takes his sovereign right to place his people in particular churches, according to his overall plan. Our God insists that we see our lives and our service *in the context of the particular church family to which he appoints us.* Verses such as this place great emphasis on a group of people being edified together, so that they relate together in love, mutual care and dedicated service for the Lord, showing forth God's power and grace.

In the light of the fact that the New Testament urges us to have a high view of the local church, how is it that so many evangelical believers have come to take such a low view? One possible reason is that they misunderstand our evangelical rejection of earthly church power. They notice that we repudiate human domination, such as church government by centralised councils or hierarchies, and that we shun human priesthood, emphasising instead the priesthood of all believers, and the direct access to the Saviour for all who seek him. However, they carry the liberty of individual believers too far, and come to think that the believer should not subordinate himself in any way to a church. They see no obligation at all, regarding the congregation as nothing more than a practical arrangement to facilitate worship and instruction.

Obviously, if the local church is no more than this, then it has no more claim upon anyone's allegiance than a school or university or supermarket or bank. As long as believers contribute towards the benefits they receive, they should not be inconvenienced or required to make sacrifices for their local church.

While it is true that the local church has no dominating authority over the lives of its members (other than to apply the standards clearly announced in the Bible), God insists that his people should feel obligated to their churches in a special way, striving to worship and serve as a co-ordinated unit, a society of people called to prove him in the closest harmony. And they are to be loyal to their church until God himself calls them elsewhere by unmistakable guidance.

All this is taught in the various biblical pictures or metaphors of the church, particularly those of the body, the Temple building, and the family unit. Church members are pictured as *integral* and *irremovable* parts performing vital functions. God's special regard for the local church as a cohesive unit is to be seen in the warning of *1 Corinthians 3.16-17*, where Paul writes to that congregation: 'Know ye not that ye are the temple of God, and that the Spirit of God dwelleth in you? If any man defile *[or destroy]* the temple of God, him shall God destroy; for the temple of God is holy, which temple ye are.'

Should the believer move?

In the light of the special status and significance of a local church, the permanent move of a believer from one church to another should only take place as the result of the clear overruling guidance of God. Later in this chapter we shall consider when loyalty is wrong, but in normal circumstances the believer's first thought must always be, 'God has called me to be loyal to my present community. Can I therefore be sure that it is his will that I should move? Am I really being called somewhere else? Is there clear evidence of his leading, supported by circumstantial guidance and having taken account of the counsel of my brothers and sisters in the Lord?'

Often Christian people are closely attached to their church, making a valuable contribution, but then a practical problem arises which appears to make moving necessary. It may be that their firm is moving to another town, or that employment prospects are much better somewhere else, or that their present area is prohibitively expensive for housing, and prices are much lower in another region of the country. None of these problems should *immediately* lead us to feel that moving is the only solution. One of the great assurances of the Christian life is that although we are frequently tried and tested by problems, often seemingly insurmountable ones, when we turn to God in prayer, he intervenes and helps us. The history of grace is a story of wonderful, often astounding, provisions from the Lord. However, some believers, the moment a problem arises of the kind mentioned, assume that it can be resolved only by uprooting and moving. They panic, and see only radical solutions, and they do not seriously ask the Lord to provide for them so that they can remain loyal to their church work. All this is very sad, with churches receiving heavy blows because members do not attempt to prove their Lord.

Some pastors have felt this very keenly, especially those ministering in new towns or inner-city areas into which Christian people hardly ever seem to move, but out of which they move very readily. Many churches in these areas 'generate' converted souls for the churches of other places, while they themselves remain as struggling causes. Did the Lord design it that way? Did he intend that his people should be totally dominated by practical problems?

Obviously, we must not expound loyalty in such a way as to obstruct the ways of God. We recognise that the sovereign Lord may move his people from one church to another. He is our heavenly General who knows the whole battlefield and all his various outposts or churches along the front line. He may call people who are settled in one church to uproot and transfer to another. In the New Testament we see the Lord moving his servants from one place to another, sometimes by sweeping large numbers out of communities by persecution, and sometimes by other means.

As a general rule, when circumstances arise which could remove us from our church, our first assumption should be that the Lord intends us to prove him where we are. It is only after we have sincerely sought a solution, and exhausted all reasonable possibilities, that we should become seriously open to moving away. How can we expect to be led in the 'right way', if we have no respect for the Lord's revealed priorities? The seeking of guidance must be rooted in a biblical value system, and this includes the duty of loyalty and commitment to the congregation in which God has set us.

Encouraging loyalty

Two concepts arising out of the expression 'the body of Christ' should help us to develop the supportive, devoted attitude which we ought to have for our local church. This magnificent term (used in *1 Corinthians 12.27*) may refer in Scripture both to the entire, world-wide Church of Christ, and to an individual congregation. As we have seen, the term speaks of a harmonious, closely organised unit, with interdependent parts and limbs. But it also speaks of a person's *presence*. Just as we are present in a place when our body is there, so Christ is seen in the world by his church. Every (spiritual) local church is his representative body in the world.

Surely, then, the local church, as his representative body, must be treated with the utmost respect and consideration. As members, *we* are the body of Christ! Whatever we do for his representative body, we do for him and to him. Whatever we fail to do for the church, we fail to do for him. If I am lazy or indifferent toward my church – the body of Christ   I am lazy and indifferent to him. If I am disloyal to his body, I am disloyal to him. How can I hurt the body of Christ, or abuse it? How can I lightly leave or forsake it?

To further stir our loyalty to the local church there is a second idea suggested by the term 'body of Christ'. It is that of the *sanctity of life*. The word 'body' reminds us that the local church is a living thing. Supposing we see a person lying in the street, injured and bleeding; what do we do? Do we just pass by? If we do, we will afterwards feel sick and desperately ashamed, because there is within everyone a powerful respect for life, and we cannot betray that instinctual responsibility for the preserving of life without paying a price.

As Christians, we should possess a similar instinct for the health and well-being of the body of Christ, the local church. Viewed spiritually, it is a precious, living body, Christ being alive in its members, having bound them together to represent him in the world. How can we allow it to be hurt? How can we bear to see limbs torn out? The world allows and encourages abortion, which is an outrage against the sanctity of human life, but the indifference shown by some believers to the body of Christ is to some degree a similar outrage in the spiritual realm.

When church members uproot and move as though their place in the body of Christ is of no significance, it is because they have lost their sense of awe and respect for the local church as the body of Christ. What a precious and important thing the congregation is! It is far, far more than a 'convenient arrangement'. It is something to which we owe special love, loyalty and service, so long as it remains a worthy church.

Wrong motives for leaving

When the next trial arises in our lives, will we have the right priorities? In *Romans 16.10* Paul salutes Apelles, who was 'approved in Christ', which means that he had gained the victory in a great test or trial. He had come through that trial on the Lord's side, proving his power in his situation. Many fall in the time of trial without even a struggle, and consequently they may suffer years of unhappiness without real spiritual usefulness. Some have gone into a spiritual wilderness because matters of career or location became the biggest influence in their lives, causing them to abandon their place in the service of the Lord.

In times of trial or decision, we need to search our hearts to see what desires are really influencing us. We know of people who have moved from the inner city because they did not care for built-up areas, and longed for green fields and beauty. The assumption of these friends was that other Christian city-dwellers adored the polluted air and grimy buildings. Clearly if all members of inner-city churches followed the natural desire to flee to more pleasant districts there would be no evangelical churches left in our most densely populated areas.

Countless Christians stand fast in other undesirable and unattractive locations, remaining for the sake of their local church and its testimony. Where in the Bible do we read that the first rule of guidance is that we are to seek the most congenial and attractive surroundings? It is the worldling who makes his own pleasure and enjoyment his first priority, but we are to stay or go wherever the Lord positions us, realising that trials and temptations await us in an 'Eden' just as much as in a 'Babylon'.

There are other factors also which carry people away from their churches unnecessarily. Every pastor has experience of members who have moved away from their fellowship because they had some besetting weakness they would not control. Their spiritual lives suffered, they became unhappy, and eventually decided that the fault was not in them but in their church. They began to sulk and complain, and soon became convinced that they were not receiving spiritual food, help or fellowship. Eventually they left the church, but not because the Lord had led them on. A high and worthy view of the local church may have helped them not to turn against their church, but they did not have such a view, and the church soon became a punch-bag for the release of tensions and dissatisfaction.

C. H. Spurgeon may well have been describing this in *Sermons in Candles*. Alongside an engraving of a very odd-shaped candle, unable to fit into any holder or stand, he wrote:

I know persons who cannot get on anywhere; but, according to their own belief, the fault is not in themselves, but in their surroundings. I could sketch you a brother who is unable to do any good because all the churches are so faulty. He was once with *us*, but he came to know us too well, and grew disgusted with our dogmatism and want of taste. He went to the Independents who have so much more culture, breadth, and liberality. He grew weary of what he called 'cold dignity'. He wanted more fire, and therefore favoured the Methodists with his patronage. Alas! he did not find them the flaming zealots he had supposed them to be: he very soon outgrew both them and their doctrines, and joined our most excellent friends, the Presbyterians.

These proved to be by far too high and dry for him, and he became rather sweet upon the Swedenborgians, and would have joined them had not his wife led him among the Episcopalians. Here he might have enjoyed the *optium cum dignitate*, have taken it easy with admirable propriety, and have even grown into a churchwarden; but he was not content; and before long I heard that he was an Exclusive Brother!

There I leave him, hoping that he may be better in his new line than he has ever been in the old ones. 'The course of nature could no further go': if he has not fallen among a loving united people now, where will he find them? Yet I expect that as Adam left Paradise so will he ultimately fall from his high estate.

An unsettled member's heart-searching must be ready to unearth unsavoury motives. Why would we want to leave our church? Sometimes people become disenchanted through thinking of themselves more highly than they ought to think, becoming very upset because their perceived talents are not sufficiently recognised, and they are not given early respect or office. They soon think they will be much better off in another (much 'better') church, and having lost their biblical loyalty, they may eventually make their move.

When loyalty is challenged

Although some people have failed in their loyalty to their church, countless others have proved the Lord in a marvellous way. The practice of loyalty to *biblical priorities* has brought them a series of wonderful provisions and blessings. Over the years we have heard often of accommodation being found, mortgages becoming unexpectedly available, employment needs being met, and a host of other provisions also. Sometimes it transpires that the Lord really is leading a believer to a new church 'posting', but often he provides so that they may stay where they are.

It may be that to remain in one's church will entail a loss of employment status, or some other cost, and we should ask ourselves, 'Am I ready for this?' We should remind ourselves that the history of the church is full of the loyal sacrifices of the Lord's people. Years ago, in time of war, men left their families to go and fight for their country, and many in fear and trembling performed heroic deeds. Many were cut down in their youth for the defence of the realm. But what cause could be more vital or glorious than that of the Lord of hosts, and the battle for everlasting souls? Yet we hear of believers who say, 'I would never put my career prospects at risk. I must do whatever my company demands, and go wherever promotion or advancement dictates.' The mighty grace of God brings new values and emotions into the life of a true convert, and we must take care not to lose these values as we go on in the Christian life. We must be *all* for Christ, and for his cause and his church.

It is good for us to keep in mind the fact that all believers at some time are likely to be subjected to the devil's attempts to shift them from the church fellowship where God has placed them. There will be many difficulties and trials for all, and the more they seek to serve the Lord, the more they will encounter them. We all need great tenacity, and a deep sense of belonging to our church. Most believers who have been especially used by God for the building up of their fellowship have at some time been subjected to intense pressures to uproot and relocate elsewhere. Perhaps these trials were given so that they might prove the Lord's provisions for them, and be all the more certain of their 'posting'. Satan is constantly trying to spoil churches by taking believers out of the 'element' in which God has placed them. He is constantly tempting God's people to seek greener pastures elsewhere.

What about those new-town young couples referred to at the beginning of this chapter, who walked out on an infant church so easily? Were they people of loyalty, commitment, sacrifice and courage? One wonders where they are now. Are they enjoying high academic or commercial positions? Are they well established in beautiful homes with fine cars parked in their driveways?

In seeking guidance, let us recognise that when the Lord sets us in a sound church, it is a divine appointment, and we must honour and respect that with all our strength. We are not free agents, and should never be moved by whims. When it is God's time to move us elsewhere, we must be fully and sincerely satisfied that he is really directing and overruling.

This chapter has said nothing about special cases, such as students, or even ministers of the Gospel. The existence of a sound church for Christian service is a key factor in choosing a college, but a study course in another city does not come within the scope of a permanent move. Ministers may be called by God from one sphere of ministry to another. We acknowledge that there are many legitimate reasons for Christians to be on the move, and the Lord is frequently the author of our moves, but the responsibility of honouring primary biblical loyalties has been too widely ignored in these days of high 'mobility', to the great hurt of churches and individuals.

When loyalty is wrong

Although loyalty to the local church is a biblical duty, there are circumstances in which loyalty is misplaced, and believers should leave. The painful irony is that some Christians show little loyalty to their church when God commands them to *cleave to it*, and amazing loyalty when God tells them to *leave it*. To know when loyalty is commanded, and when it is not, is a crucial aspect of divine guidance. Thousands of believers have remained trapped in apostate denominational churches where the Truth has long been derided and compromised, because they misunderstood loyalty and placed it before Truth.

The fact is that in his Word God constantly calls his people out of dead and unworthy churches, but numerous believers appear not to notice. They deprive themselves of sound ministry, strengthen the hands of false teachers (the Lord's enemies), and lose years of fruitful service by remaining in unsound churches. The biblical command that we should stay clear of all false teaching and apostasy is not merely negative, but is a positive and constructive act of spiritual obedience, safeguarding the true Gospel message and protecting the doctrinal purity of the people of God. The work of the Gospel is seriously hampered by the fact that many of the Lord's people are spread thinly around in compromised or completely dead and apostate churches. If they would only regroup to stand behind *sound*, Gospel-preaching churches, these would be vastly more effective. The biblical call to separate from error is God's own call to his people, and to obey it is a response of love leading to positive blessing.

Consider the many texts in which we are told not to associate with churches and ministers who deny the fundamentals of the true faith, such as the infallibility of the Bible, and the doctrine of salvation by faith alone. In *Romans 16.17* Paul commands that we 'mark them which cause divisions and offences contrary to the doctrine which ye have learned; *and avoid them*.' Should we worship and work in churches with false teachers? Should we listen to and support ministers and clergy who do not wholeheartedly believe and teach the Gospel? The inspired apostle writes: 'Though we, or an angel from heaven, preach any other gospel unto you than that which we have preached unto you, let him be accursed' *(Galatians 1.8)*. Apostate churches and preachers are (says Paul) 'the enemies of the cross of Christ' *(Philippians 3.18)*. The apostle John (in *2 John 10-11*) lays a solemn charge upon us, saying of ministers and clergy who reject true evangelical doctrine – 'If there come any unto you, and bring not this doctrine, receive him not into your house, neither bid him God speed: for he that biddeth him God speed is partaker of his evil deeds.'

Are we assisting non-evangelical teachers? Have we not realised that in God's sight we are assisting his enemies? The scriptures quoted are God's authoritative commands to us, telling us to leave wrong church connections. We should not say, 'Well, I'll think about it, and see if the Lord leads me.' He *has* led us already.

In *1 Timothy 4.1* we are warned that 'in the latter times some shall depart from the faith, giving heed to seducing spirits, and doctrines of devils.' False teaching will enter many churches, and take them over. How should true believers respond? Says Paul, 'If any man... consent not to wholesome words, even the words of our Lord Jesus Christ, and to the doctrine which is according to godliness... from such withdraw thyself' *(1 Timothy 6.3-5)*. We are to 'shun' false teaching *(2 Timothy 2.16)*.

The command to believers to keep themselves completely apart from Bible-denying error is also expressed in *2 Corinthians 6.14-17*:

'Be ye not unequally yoked together with unbelievers: for what fellowship hath righteousness with unrighteousness? and what communion hath light with darkness? and what concord hath Christ with Belial? or what part hath he that believeth with an infidel? and what agreement hath the temple of God with idols? for ye are the temple of the living God; as God hath said, I will dwell in them, and walk in them; and I will be their God, and they shall be my people. Wherefore come out from among them, and be ye separate, saith the Lord, and touch not the unclean thing; and I will receive you.'

The purpose of our reviewing these biblical passages is to show that God has already provided ample guidance on this issue. The matter is already settled for us in Scripture. If a church teaches or allows fundamental error, or associates supportively with those that do, we have a duty to appeal for repentance and correction, and if there is no response, to leave.

These scriptures apply not only to churches, but also to other Christian organisations. Should we co-operate with a Christian Union in our college or our firm if that society has non-evangelical committee members and speakers? The Bible says we should not. Should we support evangelistic crusades that have committee members and ministers on the platform who are opposed to evangelical Truth? The Bible says not. Should we support evangelists who refer their 'converts' to unsound churches? In all these matters we already have clear guidance in the Word.

When loyalty is wrong toward sound churches

Are there any circumstances in which believers ought to leave doctrinally sound churches? Sadly, there are church failings which are so serious that Christians have a duty to withdraw if the situation cannot be corrected. Even though a church may wholeheartedly believe the fundamental doctrines of the Bible, it may fall into such sin that it is no longer fit or qualified to function as a church, and no longer entitled to the loyalty of its members. We see this in the *Book of Revelation* where the church at Ephesus was told that if it did not repent of its sin it would have its 'candlestick' or 'lampstand' (its status as a true church) taken away. Here are three areas of church misconduct which involve such serious disobedience to God that dedicated Christians must withdraw – if the church refuses to address the situation:

1. First, *if a church refuses to exercise discipline* when serious offences are committed by members, then we have a duty to protest, and if the church refuses to obey God's Word, to leave it. 'Have no fellowship,' says the Lord through Paul, 'with the unfruitful works of darkness, but rather reprove them' *(Ephesians 5.11)*. The New Testament insists that the purity of the church is taken seriously, and *1 Corinthians 5* shows the necessity of this.

2. Secondly, *if a church shows no inclination to obey the great commission* and engage in Gospel work, and nothing can be done to stir it up to obedience, believers may well have a duty to leave that church. A local church must proclaim the Gospel. If this primary function is ignored, then the church forfeits the loyalty of true-hearted members. How can they be expected to waste their lives in lazy, heartless or disobedient churches? Why should they be rendered fruitless because their church is not interested in the Saviour's highest work?

3. Thirdly, *if a church ignores the standards of God's Word* by allowing the use of worldly and carnal styles of worship and evangelism, then true believers are bound to experience a great crisis of conscience. How can they cleave to a church which corrupts holy things and makes its members participate in ungodly worship contrary to *James 4.4* – 'Know ye not that the friendship of the world is enmity with God? whosoever therefore will be a friend of the world is the enemy of God.' Loyalty to the Lord and his commands in such areas certainly comes before loyalty to the local church.

All three examples mentioned here cancel out the duty of loyalty to a church, regardless of the fact that it may be sound in basic doctrine.

Where such problems do not exist, however, we must believe that God calls us to a church, and commands us to be loyal to it. We should regard ourselves as permanent limbs or parts of that body until he moves us, and have a readiness to be utterly faithful to any sound and active fellowship to which God shall call and 'post' us. The Christian life is not a life of selfish individualism, but a life to be spent as a fellow labourer and fellow soldier in that unit of believers where God intends us to be.

> *Lord, from whom all blessings flow,*
> *Perfecting the church below,*
> *Steadfast, may we cleave to thee,*
> *Love the powerful union be;*
> *Bind our willing spirits, join*
> *Each to each, and all to thine,*
> *Lead us into paths of peace,*
> *Harmony and holiness.*
>
> *Move and actuate and guide;*
> *Various gifts to each divide;*
> *Placed according to thy will*
> *Let us all our work fulfil;*
> *Never from our service move,*
> *Needful to each other prove;*
> *Use the grace on each bestowed*
> *Fashioned by the hand of God.*
>
> *Charles Wesley*

5
The Rules of Church Membership

The following principles of conduct for church members (with Scripture texts) were compiled in the 1740s by the famous John Fletcher of Madeley (1729-1785). Born in Switzerland of noble family, John Fletcher (originally de la Fléchère) was educated in Geneva, but settled in England where he was converted through the Great Awakening that began in 1739. In 1760 he was appointed Vicar of Madeley, becoming noted for his promotion of evangelism, and also godliness, genuineness and devotion among Christian people.

These brief, challenging, yet comprehensive rules (adapted and abridged from the original) sum up the whole duty of believers in their lives, and particularly in their conduct in the church.

IN THE OLD TESTAMENT we read, 'they that feared the Lord spake often one to another: and the Lord hearkened, and heard it, and a book of remembrance was written before him for them that feared the Lord, and that thought upon his name' (*Malachi 3.16*).

In the Gospels we have the account of a company of people drawn together by the Lord Jesus Christ himself. After his ascension these 'all continued with one accord in prayer and supplication' *(Acts 1.14)*.

When the Day of Pentecost came they were again 'all with one accord in one place' *(Acts 2.1)*, and after their numbers had been vastly increased by the outpouring of God's power 'they continued stedfastly in the apostles' doctrine and fellowship, and in breaking of bread, and in prayers ... And all that believed were together, and had all things common' *(Acts 2.42, 44)*.

That this close association was on no account to be laid aside is evident from the repeated commands of the apostles:

'Not forsaking the assembling of ourselves together, as the manner of some is; but exhorting one another' *(Hebrews 10.25)*.

'Let the word of Christ dwell in you richly in all wisdom; teaching and admonishing one another in psalms and hymns and spiritual songs' *(Colossians 3.16)*.

'Wherefore comfort yourselves together, and edify one another, even as also ye do ... warn them that are unruly, comfort the feeble-minded, support the weak' *(1 Thessalonians 5.11, 14)*.

Encouraged by these apostolic exhortations and the example set us by spiritual believers in every age, church members should prove their sincerity by putting on the form of godliness which is the standard laid down in the Scripture. This can be summed up under three headings:

(a) Cease to do evil *(Isaiah 1.16, Romans 12.9)*.

(b) Learn to do good *(Isaiah 1.17, Romans 12.9)*.

(c) Seek light and blessing from God by using the channels he has provided *(Isaiah 55.6, 2 Timothy 2.5)*.

Cease to do evil

1. No member should either follow or be led by the glamour and vanity of this evil world, through such things as worldly entertainment, dancing, and gambling. No Christian should follow

leisure-time activities which cannot be followed in the name of the Lord Jesus. See *Ephesians 4.22, Romans 12.2, Galatians 5.24-25, Colossians 3.17.*

2. No member should give place to softness and needless self-pampering and laziness, neither wear showy or expensive clothing. See *1 Thessalonians 5.23, 1 Peter 2.11, 2 Timothy 2.3, 1 Corinthians 9.27.*

3. No member should take part in unprofitable or unkind conversation, much less shall he be guilty of filthy talking and joking, or speaking behind the backs of others. See *Ephesians 4.29, 5.3-4, Jude 1.8, Acts 23.5, James 4.11.*

4. No member should be found to be a busybody, or guilty of unkindness to others. See *1 Peter 3.8, 4.15, 1 Timothy 5.13.*

5. No member should sing those songs or read those books which do not tend to make him a better Christian and a better neighbour. See *James 5.13, Ephesians 2.3, Colossians 3.16.*

6. No member should profane the day of the Lord by buying or selling or doing such things as can be done on Saturday or left undone until Monday. See fourth commandment, *Isaiah 58.13, Numbers 15.32-36.*

7. No member should be guilty of uncleanness or drunkenness. See *Romans 13.13, Matthew 24.36-51, 1 Thessalonians 5.6-8.*

8. No member should fight, quarrel, brawl, return evil for evil, shouting for shouting, nor insult for insult. See sixth commandment, *1 Corinthians 5.11, 6.7, Romans 13.13.*

9. No member should make profit in business at the expense of others, or do things to others that he would object to them doing to him. See *1 Thessalonians 4.6, 1 Corinthians 10.24, Romans 13.7.*

10. No member should follow spiritual things at the expense of

his proper duties and work. The time to be spent in Christian things shall be taken from his leisure or saved from his sleep and not stolen from his work or duties. See *2 Thessalonians 3.8-12, 1 Timothy 5.14, Romans 12.11*.

Learn to do good

1. Every member should minister to the physical requirements of others by providing for those in need; visiting the sick, and helping those in trouble. See *Ecclesiastes 4.10, Galatians 6.2* and *10, Matthew 25.35*, etc, *James 1.27*.

2. Every member should minister to the souls of others according to his power, by patiently talking to the ignorant about spiritual things, gently reproving the profane, and carefully warning those who walk in sin, as opportunities arise. See *Leviticus 19, Deuteronomy 6.7, Hebrews 3.13*.

3. Every member should do all within his power to reprove the immoral and abandoned conduct of those around him by the testimony of his own, well-ordered, commendable life. See *Ephesians 5.11, 1 Samuel 3.13, James 5.19* and *20*.

4. Every member should be unusually diligent in business life. See *Matthew 5.16, 1 Peter 2.12, 2 Corinthians 6.3*.

5. Every member should deny himself, take up his cross daily, and follow Christ as a born-again man, submitting to the reproach of the Gospel and expecting that, for his Lord's sake, men will say all manner of evil against him just as they did of the Lord. See *Matthew 16.24*.

Seek blessing from God's appointed channels

1. Every member must attend the worship of God in the church. See *Psalm 42.4, Luke 2.37*.

2. Every member must hear the Word of God taught and expounded. See *2 Timothy 4.2, Romans 10.17*.

3. Every member must take part in the Lord's Supper at every opportunity. See *Acts 2.46, 1 Corinthians 11.24.*

4. Every member who is a parent must minister to his family and nourish his children in the faith. See *Exodus 13.8-10, 14-16, Deuteronomy 6.6-9, Proverbs 22.6, Matthew 19.14.*

5. Every member must engage in private prayer at least night and morning. See *Psalm 119.164, Daniel 6.13, Acts 9.11, Matthew 14.23.*

6. Every member must read the Scriptures regularly, and meditate upon them. See *Deuteronomy 6.7, Psalm 1.2, Revelation 1.3, John 5.39, Luke 10.26, Acts 17.11.*

It is God's command, that if any man who is called a brother is promiscuous, or a covetous person, or a contentious, insulting person, or a drunkard, we ought not to keep company with him, not even to eat with him. See *1 Corinthians 5.11.*

A disorderly, idle, worldly disposition, or a proud, fiercely argumentative temperament (the greatest enemy of the church's peace and love) should be disciplined, remembering that Paul said, 'Have no company with him, that he may be ashamed. Yet count him not as an enemy, but admonish him as a brother' *(2 Thessalonians 3.14-15).*

Members should be on the watch for any ill-feelings towards one another, and if such feelings are within them they must state them without delay. See *Romans 12.9, Philippians 2.1-3, Matthew 18.15-17.*

Members must be particularly careful not to rest with an outward form of godliness, but to seek the power of it and to seek also the humbling love of God to be shed abroad in their hearts.

They must be 'kindly affectioned one to another...in honour preferring one another' *(Romans 12.10).* 'Rejoice with them that do rejoice, and weep with them that weep. Be of the same mind one toward another. Mind not high things, but condescend to men of low estate. Be not wise in your own conceits' *(Romans 12.15-16).*

6
The Family Covenant

This famous pledge of spiritual oneness was the *Solemn Covenant* adopted by the London congregation of Pastor Benjamin Keach (the Horsleydown Baptist Meeting), around 1689. In time this church became the Metropolitan Tabernacle, in which new members subscribe still to this great summary of Christian duty. In the seventeenth century this Covenant would be read out at the beginning of every Lord's Supper service. It serves today as a very beautiful reminder of what the Lord requires in sincere believers.

WE WHO DESIRE TO WALK together in the fear of the Lord, do, through the assistance of his Holy Spirit, profess our deep and serious humiliation for all our transgressions.

And we do solemnly, in the presence of God and of each other, in the sense of our own unworthiness, give up ourselves to the Lord in a church state, according to the apostolic constitution, that he may be our God, and we may be his people, through the everlasting covenant of his free grace, in which alone we hope to be accepted by him, through his blessed Son Jesus Christ, whom we take to be our High Priest, to justify and sanctify us, and our Prophet to teach us; and to be subject to him as our Lawgiver, and the King of Saints; and to conform to all his holy laws and ordinances, for our growth, establishment, and consolation; that we may be as a holy spouse unto him, and serve him in our generation, and wait for his second appearance, as our glorious Bridegroom.

Being fully satisfied in the way of church communion, and the truth of grace in some good measure upon one another's spirits, we do solemnly join ourselves together in a holy union and fellowship, humbly submitting to the discipline of the Gospel, and all holy duties required of a people in such a spiritual relation.

1. We do promise and engage to walk in all holiness, godliness, humility, and brotherly love, as much as in us lieth to render our communion delightful to God, comfortable to ourselves, and lovely to the rest of the Lord's people.

2. We do promise to watch over each other's conversations, and not to suffer sin upon one another, so far as God shall discover it to us, or any of us; and to stir up one another to love and good works; to warn, rebuke, and admonish one another with meekness, according to the rules left to us of Christ in that behalf.

3. We do promise in a special manner to pray for one another, and for the glory and increase of this church, and for the presence of God in it, and the pouring forth of his Spirit on it, and his protection over it to his glory.

4. We do promise to bear one another's burdens, to cleave to one another, and to have a fellow-feeling with one another, in all conditions both outward and inward, as God in his providence shall cast any of us into.

5.   We do promise to bear with one another's weaknesses, failings, and infirmities, with much tenderness, not discovering them to any without the church, nor any within, unless according to Christ's rule, and the order of the Gospel provided in that case.

6.   We do promise to strive together for the truth of the Gospel and purity of God's ways and ordinances, to avoid causes and causers of division, endeavouring to keep the unity of the Spirit in the bond of peace *(Ephesians 4.3)*.

7.   We do promise to meet together on Lord's Days, and at other times, as the Lord shall give us opportunities, to serve and glorify God in the way of his worship, to edify one another, and to contrive the good of his church.

8.   We do promise according to our ability (or as God shall bless us with the good things of this world) to communicate to our pastor or minister, God having ordained that they that preach the Gospel should live of the Gospel.

And now can anything lay a greater obligation upon the conscience than this covenant, what then is the sin of such who violate it?

These and all other Gospel duties we humbly submit unto, promising and purposing to perform, not in our own strength, being conscious of our own weakness, but in the power and strength of the blessed God, whose we are, and whom we desire to serve. To whom be glory now and for evermore. Amen.

The Faith
Great Christian Truths
119 pages, paperback, ISBN 1 978 870855 54 9

There is nothing like this popular, non-technical sweep through key themes of the Christian faith, highlighting very many inspiring and enlivening points. It often takes an unusual approach to a topic in order to bring out the full wonder and significance. It is designed to be enjoyed by seasoned Christians, and also by all who want to explore the great features of the faith, and discover the life of the soul.

CONTENTS:

The Mysterious Nature of a Soul	The New Birth
What God is Actually Like	Why the Resurrection?
The Fall of Man	Prophecies of Resurrection
The Three Dark Hours of Calvary	The Holy Trinity

Faith, Doubts, Trials and Assurance
139 pages, paperback, ISBN 1 978 870855 50 1

Ongoing faith is essential for answered prayer, effective service, spiritual stability and real communion with God. In this book many questions are answered about faith, such as –

How may we assess the state of our faith? How can faith be strengthened? What are the most dangerous doubts? How should difficult doubts be handled? What is the biblical attitude to trials? How can we tell if troubles are intended to chastise or to refine? What can be done to obtain assurance? What are the sources of assurance? Can a believer commit the unpardonable sin? Exactly how is the Lord's presence felt?

Dr Masters provides answers, with much pastoral advice, drawing on Scripture throughout.

Do We Have a Policy?
Paul's Ten Point Policy for Church Health & Growth
119 pages, paperback, ISBN 1 978 870855 30 3

What are our aims for the shaping of our church fellowship, and for its growth? Do we have an agenda or framework of desired objectives? The apostle Paul had a very definite policy, and called it his 'purpose', using a Greek word which means – a plan or strategy displayed for all to see.

This book sets out ten policy ideals, gleaned from Paul's teaching, all of which are essential for the health and growth of a congregation today.

Not Like Any Other Book
Interpreting the Bible
161 pages, paperback, ISBN 978 1 870855 43 3

Faulty Bible interpretation lies at the root of every major mistake and 'ism' assailing churches today, and countless Christians are asking for the old, traditional and proven way of handling the Bible to be spelled out plainly.

A new approach to interpretation has also gripped many evangelical seminaries and Bible colleges, an approach based on the ideas of unbelieving critics, stripping the Bible of God's message, and leaving pastors impoverished in their preaching.

This book reveals what is happening, providing many brief examples of right and wrong interpretation. The author shows that the Bible includes its own rules of interpretation, and every believer should know what these are.

The Lord's Pattern for Prayer
118 pages, paperback, ISBN 978 1 870855 36 5

Subtitled – 'Studying the lessons and spiritual encouragements in the most famous of all prayers.' This volume is almost a manual on prayer, providing a real spur to the devotional life. The Lord's own plan and agenda for prayer – carefully amplified – takes us into the presence of the Father, to prove the privileges and power of God's promises to those who pray.

Chapters cover each petition in the Lord's Prayer. Here, too, are sections on remedies for problems in prayer, how to intercede for others, the reasons why God keeps us waiting for answers, and the nature of the prayer of faith.

God's Rules for Holiness
Unlocking the Ten Commandments
139 pages, paperback, ISBN 978 1 870855 37 2

Taken at face value the Ten Commandments are binding on all people, and will guard the way to Heaven, so that evil will never spoil its glory and purity. But the Commandments are far greater than their surface meaning, as this book shows.

They challenge us as Christians on a still wider range of sinful deeds and attitudes. They provide positive virtues as goals. And they give immense help for staying close to the Lord in our walk and worship.

The Commandments are vital for godly living and for greater blessing, but we need to enter into the panoramic view they provide for the standards and goals for redeemed people.

Worship in the Melting Pot

148 pages, paperback, ISBN 978 1 870855 33 4

'Worship is truly in the melting pot,' says the author. 'A new style of praise has swept into evangelical life shaking to the foundations traditional concepts and attitudes.' How should we react? Is it all just a matter of taste and age? Will churches be helped, or changed beyond recognition?

This book presents four essential principles which Jesus Christ laid down for worship, and by which every new idea must be judged.

Here also is a fascinating view of how they worshipped in Bible times, including their rules for the use of instruments, and the question is answered – What does the Bible teach about the content and order of a service of worship today?

The Baptist Confession of Faith of 1689

Updated with notes by Peter Masters

53 pages, paperback, ISBN 978 1 870855 24 2

C. H. Spurgeon said of this great Confession – 'Here the youngest members of our church will have a body of Truth in small compass, and by means of the scriptural proofs, will be able to give a reason of the hope that is in them.'

This brilliant summary of doctrine (in the same family as the Westminster Confession), with its invaluable proof texts, is here gently modernised in punctuation, with archaic words replaced. Explanations of difficult phrases have been added in italic brackets. A brief history of the Confession, with an index, is included.

For other Wakeman titles please see www.wakemantrust.org

Stand for the Truth

This gives the biblical arguments for separation from false teaching, showing the positive value of this. Ten commonly-heard arguments in defence of 'inclusivism' (co-operation with Bible-denying groups in, for example, evangelism) are answered.

Are We Fundamentalists?

A new version of evangelicalism has emerged over the last 40 years, quite different from the old. The old is biblical; the new is full of compromise. This explains the differences, and shows the importance of being a contender for the faith.

Your Reasonable Service in the Lord's Work

Designed to inspire church members to seek avenues of service within the church, this focuses on the strong exhortations to Christian service in the New Testament. A call to embrace the concept of a working church.

The Goal of Brotherly Love

The great goal is *Philadelphia* love – a tenacity of love equal to the love of a blood tie. What obstructs this among believers? What steps must be taken to promote and preserve it?

Tithing

Subtitled – The Privilege of Christian Stewardship. The biblical principles presented under a series of helpful headings. Many questions are answered.

The Power of Prayer Meetings

Shows why corporate prayer is commanded by Christ and given unique promises. Includes practical advice on the form of the meeting, and the style and content of prayer. An appendix shows why women should participate.

The Purposes of the Lord's Supper

Nine purposes behind the Lord's Supper, providing a basis for thought and prayer at the Table.

Baptism – the Picture and its Purpose

Describes the fourfold pictorial message of baptism intended by God for the believer, the church, and the world. Also offers biblical reasons why baptism is for believers only, by immersion.

Seven Certain Signs of True Conversion

Are there recognisable signs that true conversion has occurred? How can seekers tell if God has worked in their hearts? How can Christian workers discern the spiritual standing of a seeker or inquirer, or an applicant for baptism and church membership? A guide to the marks of true salvation.

21-36 page booklets; available from www.tabernaclebookshop.org